MW00415438

365
Ways to
get Rich

Birgit Willberger
Joachim Tack

DUMONT
monte

Text: Birgit Willberger, Joachim Tack
Translation: Kirsten Marxen
Copy editing: APE Overath
Cover design: BOROS, Wuppertal
Cover photograph (centre): Tai Pan © 1995 Lenz + Partner GmbH
Cover photograph (right): © laif, Cologne

© 2000 DuMontmonte UK, London

ISBN 3-7701-7008-3
Printed in Slovenia

1

You don't get rich from the money you earn, you get rich from the money you don't spend.

Henry Ford I

... especially when it is invested wisely.

2

Don't make excuses for not having made more out of your money.

Whether you begin with 15 £, 30 £ or 300 £ a month,

the amount that you start with is not decisive;

it is important only that you start.

Otherwise, in your later years you will look back on

a lifetime of missed opportunities.

3

If friends or acquaintances offer you tips about how to earn a lot of money fast, take care. In many cases, these are offers that don't pan out. Serious offers are always up front and never under the counter as a "secret tip".

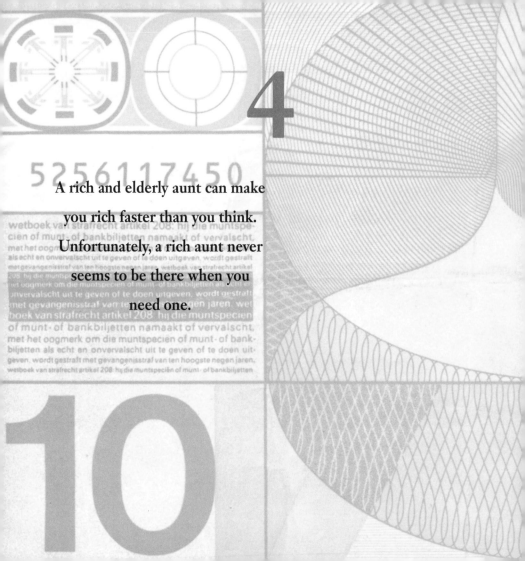

5 2 5 6 1 1 7 4 5 0

A rich and elderly aunt can make
you rich faster than you think.
Unfortunately, a rich aunt never
seems to be there when you
need one.

wetboek van strafrecht artikel 208: hij die muntspecien of munt- of bankbiljetten namaakt of vervalscht,
met het oogmerk om die muntspecien of munt- of bank-
als echt en onvervalscht uit te geven of te doen uitgeven, wordt gestraft
met gevangenisstraf van ten hoogste negen jaren. wetboek van strafrecht artikel
208: hij die muntspecien of munt- of bankbiljetten als echt en
met oogmerk om die muntspecien of munt- of bankbiljetten als echt en
onvervalscht uit te geven of te doen uitgeven, wordt gestraft
met gevangenisstraf van ten hoogste negen jaren. wetboek van strafrecht artikel 208: hij die muntspecien
of munt- of bankbiljetten namaakt of vervalscht,
met het oogmerk om die muntspecien of munt- of bankbiljetten als echt en onvervalscht uit te geven of te doen uitgeven, wordt gestraft met gevangenisstraf van ten hoogste negen jaren.
wetboek van strafrecht artikel 208: hij die muntspecien of munt- of bankbiljetten

5

Never ask what the government or
your country can do for you—ask instead what
you can do for yourself.

52561174

6

Reject the standard products of banks and
advisors. You are an individual,
and you have a right to individually tailored
investment suggestions.

If you don't want to give away money, use your giro account only for short-term and daily business transactions, and transfer any excess amount to other forms of investment with a better interest rate so that it can grow.

7

8

The smaller the return on an investment, the less you will earn with it or the longer it will take you to realise your saving goal. It makes sense to think about the right form of investment before you actually invest.

9

Life insurance, pension insurance funds and unit-linked
life assurances for targeted capital formation have been outdated
for a long time. The intentional obscurity of this
form of investment costs you a lot of money in the long run.
Although returns between 4% and 6.5% are advertised,
they are actually most often just at 4%.

10

To avoid running into trouble,
the rookie shareholder should start by training with
standard securities before investing in sectors
or following up on "hot tips".

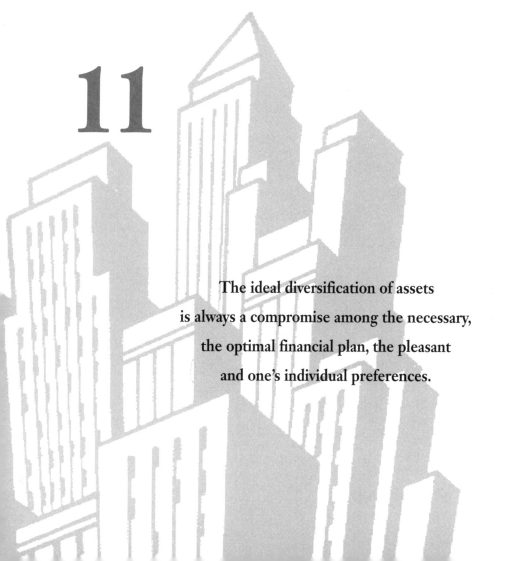

11

The ideal diversification of assets
is always a compromise among the necessary,
the optimal financial plan, the pleasant
and one's individual preferences.

12

Do you want to become wealthy? If so, it isn't enough to save a bit or do it grudgingly. Instead, you must completely restruture your investment approach!

13

If you found or join an investment club,
you will learn how to make more out of
your money in an informal way
with kindred spirits.

14

The more information you have about the diversity of the investment market, the higher the returns that you can achieve through targeted investments in the markets.

15

If parents begin saving 100 £ for their child monthly
starting in the child's first year, at an interest rate of 3% the
child will have 58,261 £ at his or her disposal after
30 years. If the 100 £ are
invested at 12% interest,
however, the child
will have access
to 311,419 £
after 30 years.

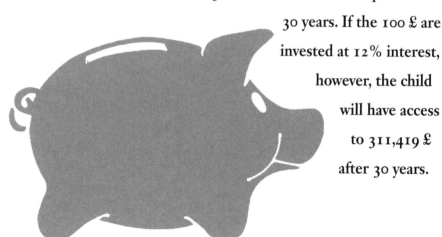

16

The saying goes, big money associates with big money.
Put a 500 £ note into your purse so that it will multiply.

17

Never buy real estate only to save taxes. Most important when buying is to assess the location, the realistic value, the potential for letting and the recovery value of a property. Only then is there a possibility that its value will increase.

18

Equity funds are ideal if you do not want to occupy yourself with the stock exchange in great detail, but would like to achieve better revenues than with bonds.

19

The success of an investment in unit trusts largely depends on the fees. Keep an eye on them!

20

The respective risk for individual investment
forms is known.
What cannot be determined exactly
is the exact point in time of losses or price
fluctuations—hence, the uncertainty.

21

In order to get a feel for the price fluctuations of shares,
make time to browse through the chart report regularly.

22

An investment without planning and strategy is pure gambling. This strategy can be successful with beginner's luck, but in the worst case, you can lose all your money.

23

Only a targeted diversification of the varied possibilities
of the investment market protects you from
big surprises and financial losses.

Le Secrétaire G^{al}

Le Contrôleur G^{al}

Le Caissier G^{al}

24

With shares, you should be less interested in a quick profit
than in the possibility to increase your investment over
the long term.

25

Day-to-day accounts
are an ideal alternative
to savings deposits,
fixed-term deposits and
government savings
bonds.

26

When investing in fixed-interest securities, pay attention to the
credit standing of the issuer, the price and currency fluctuations
because they make this form of investment risky
and can even lead to complete loss of the sum invested.

27

Diversification is the single best method
of lowering your overall investment risk.

28

Many people's best strategy for realising the dream of becoming a millionaire is to play the lottery. Save the money you would spend each week and invest it in equity funds instead—your profit is guaranteed.

29

Don't run after money,
but meet it as it approaches you.

30

Don't rely on the "hot tips" of
individual stock exchange broadcasts, journals or gurus.
Instead, gather comprehensive information and
look for shares that have sound prospects for a
long-term increase in value.
Do decide according to your feelings.

The London Stock Exchange deters small orders by demanding high fees of up to 5% or more of the order volume. It is in your interest to use other, less expensive markets for small orders.

31

The more diversified your investments,
the more certain
the increase in their value.

32

33

Funds are the most diverse and most variable form of investment.
However, just as with individual shares, their success depends
on making the correct selection.

34

Provide for the basic needs of your family and ensure the income necessary to maintain your lifestyle—these are preconditions for a targeted development of a fortune with the remaining available funds.

35

Financial and investment planning is the key to success. The earlier you realise this, the faster you will achieve financial independence.

36

Real estate purchased to let can create substantial problems. In addition to the possibility of not finding tenants or having tenants who don't pay, the much-touted tax breaks are generally much lower in reality than in theory. If after 10 years you come to the conclusion that the house is worth less than what you paid for it, your investment has become a nightmare.

37

Personal financial planning is the best basis for an individual investment strategy.

38

Insuring yourself against occupational disability
is an absolute must!
A loss of your capacity to work entails the
loss of your retirement pension plan.

39

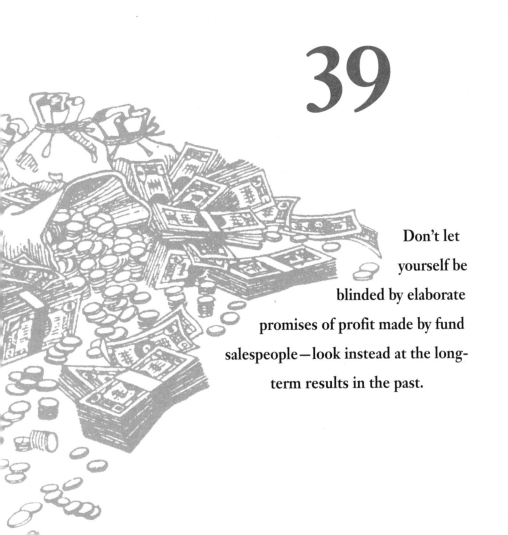

Don't let yourself be blinded by elaborate promises of profit made by fund salespeople—look instead at the long-term results in the past.

40

The risk of fraud in the investment sector has become very high.

There is such a tremendous variety of fraudulent schemes

that you often only realise the deception

after all of your invested capital is lost.

41

One of the real advantages
of unit trusts is that they require
very little of your time.

Paul Cézanne
18 – 6

42

If you rely on your government pension, you will
probably not be able to afford much. With a well planned
investment program you can enjoy life in your old age.

100 Cent Francs

E 012029158

43

Ninety percent of the players on the stock market are emotional gamblers without any idea of theory, who have no strategy.
André Kostolany

100

44

Investing in funds at a bank
is a double-edged sword.
Consider cooperating with a bank only
if it offers capable advisory service
and an extensive selection of funds.

How do you beat a stock market index?

Simple:

Early in the year, invest in the titles
with the highest dividend yield, and
hold them until the end of the year.

This strategy has actually been
successful for many years.

45

46

If you are venturesome, take a look at the so-called basket certificates, which apply to previously defined, most often theme-related baskets of shares.

47

There is no investment company
that has nothing but excellent funds.
You must make the effort to search out the interesting funds
in various investment companies.

Akzo Nobel	42.00G	41.50G	Condomi#
Alcoa	32.00G	32.00G	CompuGroup
Amazon.com	46.30G	49.00b	DAB#
American Express	55.50-T	...G	Debitel #
Amgen	70.50G	...b	Dolerit Basalt#
AOL	56.30G	...b	Dom-Brauerei
Apple Comp.	96.00G	93.80bB	Dt. Bet.#
AT&T	35.50G	36.00b	Dt. Steinz. Ffm#
Bell Atlantic Ffm	60.00-T	59.00T	Didier
Bell South Ffm	49.00-T	50.00T	Dyckerh. St.#
BP Amoco	9.70G	9.50G	Eifelhöhenklinik#
Boeing	40.50G	42.00b	Eisenhüttenwerk# 1
British Airways	5.80G	5.80G	Eurobike**
Bull	10.00G	10.00G	Eurohypo**
Canon	47.40G	47.00b	F + G#
Caterpillar	37.00G	39.50G	Ford Werke*
Cisco Systems	70.00G	69.01b	Gerling Allg.
Citigroup	66.50G	67.00b	Gerry Web.St.**
Coca Cola	56.50G	57.50b	Gerry Web.Vz.**
Compaq	28.00G	29.00b	Gildemeister #
Dell Computer	51.00B	49.80b	Henkel St.#
Disney	43.50G	44.50b	Herlitz St.#
Dow Chemical	36.00-T	36.66-T	Herlitz Vz.#
DSM	34.30G	34.80G	

48

Only invest money in shares that you can easily do without for the next few years.

20.00G	20.30G	Rheinboden#	1.41	25.01bG	24.00(
20.50TB	21.00-T	Rhein-Hyp#	39.70	540.00G	540.00
35.00TG	32.50G	Rhenag	7.67	740.00TB	769.90
37.00G	37.01G	RWE Vz.**		30.40b	31.00b
3.60G	3.55G	RWE-DEA#		195.00G	195.00
64.75b	64.00B	Salamander#	0.26	12.21G	11.500
36.70G	38.00G	Salzgitter#	0.38	7.55G	7.60G
3.85xD	4.10B	SAP St.#	1.57	509.90b	511.50
50.00G	50.00G	Springer	13.29	1150.00-T	1150.0
29.50G	28.55G	Spütz	2.00	10.80G	11.20b
4.85G	4.85G	Stollwerck		650.00B	650.00
300.00G	298.00G	Strabag#		40.00G	40.00b
12.70bB	12.75b	Ver.Dt.Nick.#		20.00G	21.00b
34.00G	33.00G	Verseidag St.#		19.81G	19.81G
57.00G	157.00G	VEW	5.11	200.00TG	191.00
310.00G	310.00G	Victoria Vers.	8.18	1290.00G	1280.0
125.00G	124.00G	Villeroy Vz.#	0.41	9.80G	9.80G
21.30b	23.50B	Volksfürsorge#	8.95	314.00B	300.00
20.80b	20.95b	VTG Lehnkering#	0.61	11.70G	11.80G
8.90G	8.80G	VW Vz.#	0.83	25.85b	26.50b
65.00G	56.11b	Wanderer		80.00-T	80.00-
1.00G	11.00G	Weru Ffm		270.00B	270.00
0.50B	10.50G	WMF Vz.#	0.64	13.80B	13.50G

49

Some of the newest creations on the financial market are funds or certificates in the B2B (business-to-business) branch.

If you work all day long, you do not have time to earn money. Set aside an hour a day to consider your finances.

50

51

Japan remains the second richest country on earth. Invest in Japanese small-cap funds, and don't hesitate to sell them once you have made a comfortable profit. ·

52

Real estate investments in foreign countries
can also be interesting and profitable.

53

Art is not profitable as an investment in most cases.

54

Investing in Asia is a must for the globally oriented European investor! Investment funds are the safest and most comfortable option.

55

Don't trade with contracts on pork bellies.

Speculating with shares is thrilling enough!

56

The fastest way to get rich?

Very simple:

Marry someone who already is.

57

Fund savings plans are a speedy route
to a fortune! With an investment of just
30 £ a month, you can profit from the above
average returns on international equity funds.
Over 30 years, your 30 £ sums can grow to
a remarkable capital of 100.000 £,
from which you can earn an additional pension
of about 650 £ monthly.

58

Equity funds can't be beat as
a long-term investment, even after
you adjust for inflation and
deduct taxes.

59

The hunt for the (seemingly) highest interest rate,

the bet on an individual "hot" share

and the greedy pursuit of fast money

dominate most investment decisions—but these

strategies seldom lead to the desired success.

60

Future funds are managed by professionals.
However, sometimes even professionals are wrong,
and a profit for the investor cannot be guaranteed.

61

To leave your money in a giro account or savings account

for fear of making investment mistakes

is the biggest possible blunder.

62

If you have a large proportion of fixed-interest securities or funds,
have exceded the amount of interest you can earn tax-free, and can
afford to relinquish your funds for the next 12 years,
the Top Ten Investment Plan—a fund managed according to
Luxembourg law—would be an excellent investment for you.

63

The foundation of sensible financial planning is
knowing how much you have!

64

Trust your feelings and intuition when it comes to money!

65

Ascertain your monthly expenditures and income. Then you can see clearly which sums are available each month to invest in your growing fortune.

66

Before you insure yourself privately, assess what you will receive from the government or other sources in case of occupational disability or retirement—you could save a lot of money on unnecessary premiums.

0125874 0000152148

SENTATIF

1
ACTION

E VALEUR NOMINALE

nd S.C.A.

JN

EUR

HORS DE FRANCE

67

In the long run, shares are the best and most profitable capital investment.

68

Shrewd investors are informed about the current interest rate trend before buying fixed-interest securities and choose a maturity date accordingly in order to achieve the best results.

69

The golden rule of fixed-interest securities is:
Never invest in long-term securities when the interest rate is low
(like now), but resort to securities that are close to maturity
in order to be able to adapt to the expected
interest rate developments at any time.

If your investment gives you heartburn, it is most definitely the wrong one. Good stock exchange advice is not found in the newspaper or passed on by relatives or acquaintances, but gradually gained through a lot of experience.

71

The stock exchange is not
a one-way street!
If you think it only rises,
take care—you could receive a
nasty shock overnight.

72

Limit your losses on the stock market
by issuing a stop order. If the price
of the share reaches the limit you
designate as "stop"
it will be sold automatically.

73

Don't set the stop too close to the
momentary value of a share — the
stock might be sold prematurely due
to normal day-to-day price
fluctuations, which is not
always desirable or in
your best interests.

74

Let your profits rise as they may with shares! Just to be on the safe side, though, adjust the stop to a higher level occasionally as the value of the stock increases.

75

In tight markets, always set a buying or selling limit.
Without a limit, the order will be executed at the next available
price, making price fluctuations of as much as 30 to 40%
to your disadvantage possible.

76

Warren Buffet once said in an interview,
"Why shouldn't I invest a large part of my money in a company that
I am convinced will be making large profits even in five years?"
The corporation in question was Coca-Cola.
And the wisdom of his attitude has been confirmed,
because success also needs time.

77

Most futures funds don't pay off because opportunities for profit are reduced by the high costs and fees.

78

Warrant funds offer a special kind of thrill:
In a short period of time, they can either double or halve
your invested money !

79

Small-cap funds, turn-around funds, or even venture capital funds are suitable for investors who are not averse to risk.

80

Index funds are a specialty product that represent the composition
of certain indexes. Their managers try to fully participate
in their profit trends.

81

Umbrella funds are interesting if the offering fund company boasts an excellent management and several first-class funds.

82

The tremendous diversity of funds on the market makes it necessary to actively pursue the right selection if you want your investment to be profitable.

83

In order to successfully manage your securities yourself,
you need more than just time — experience, a certain level
of expertise and a strong interest in this hobby are also essential.

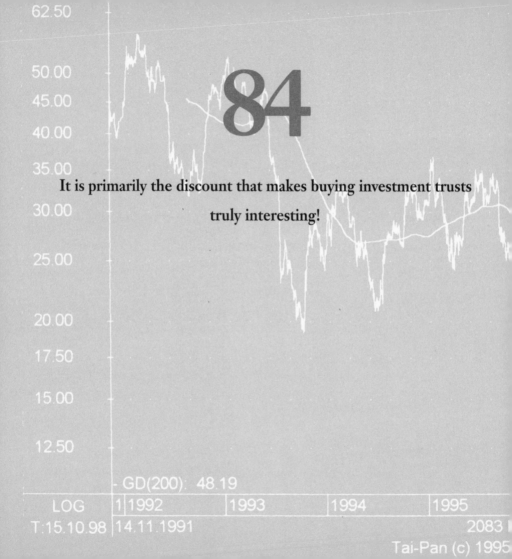

84

It is primarily the discount that makes buying investment trusts truly interesting!

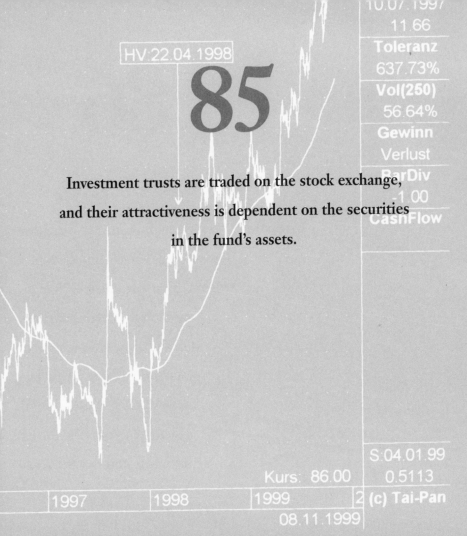

Investment trusts are traded on the stock exchange, and their attractiveness is dependent on the securities in the fund's assets.

86

If you don't have enough money to purchase
your own real estate, build your
resources at the stock exchange
over a longer period of time
in order to be able to realise
your dream later. Investing
in an open real estate fund
usually pays off only for its
initiators and not for you!

87

Hands off guarantee funds! The promised guarantee most often detracts from the expected earnings. You will never achieve a top return with them.

Kerr = Mc Gee Corporati

under the laws of the State of Delaware, therein referred t

88

8½%
JUNE 1,
2006

60000* U   1182 -C

* *CCC0093

Even in funds there are many losers.

Always pick the best from a pool of comparable funds.

* *FIFTY TH

on June 1, 2006, and to pay interest thereon from June 1, 1976, or from the most recent Interest Payment Date to which interest has been of twelve 30-day months), until the principal hereof is paid or duly provided for. The interest so payable, and punctually paid or duly provid (or one or more Predecessor Debentures, as defined in such Indenture) is registered at the close of business on the Regular Record Date for Any such interest not so punctually paid or duly provided for shall forthwith cease to be payable to the Holder on such Regular Record Da Special Record Date for the payment of such Defaulted Interest to be fixed by the Trustee, notice whereof shall be given to Holders of De ments of any securities exchange on which the Debentures may be listed, and upon such notice as may be required by such exchange, all agency of the Company maintained for that purpose in the Borough of Manhattan, The City of New York, in such coin or currency of t interest may be made at the option of the Company by check mailed to the address of the Person entitled thereto as such address shall Reference is hereby made to the further provisions of this Debenture set forth on the reverse hereof, which further provisions shall Unless the certificate of authentication hereon has been executed by or on behalf of the Trustee referred to on the reverse hereo

In Witness Whereof, Kerr = Mc Gee Corporation has caused this instrument
by its Secretary or an Assistant Secretary by his signature or a facsimile thereo

Dated: JUN 17 1976

TRUSTEE'S CERTIFICATE OF AUTHENTICATION
This is one of the Debentures referred to in the within-mentioned Indenture.
CITIBANK, N.A.,
as Trustee

By

Authorized Officer

Fund of funds are an ideal way to manage your fund assets!

The stock exchange is continuously getting faster due to better trading systems and electronics. Individual stocks also fluctuate more rapidly—in both directions. Don't panic!

91

Only funds that perform well over a long period of time will bring the promised returns.

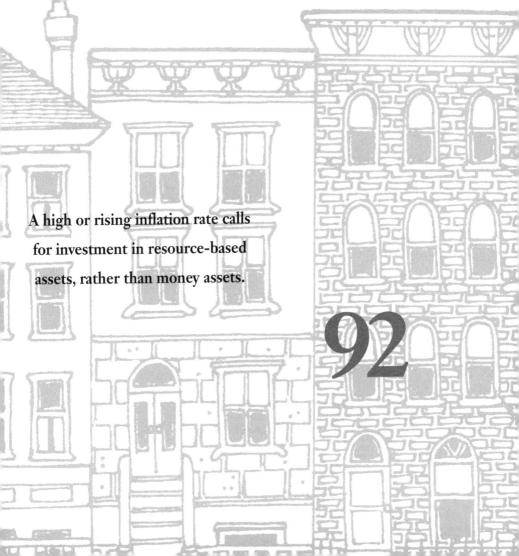

A high or rising inflation rate calls for investment in resource-based assets, rather than money assets.

92

93

You can only become rich if you have enough
money to be able to invest some. To ensure
that this is always the case, you need disability
and income insurance.

94

If you can sleep well at night
after making an investment
decision, it was the right
decision.

95

Trading shares outside the market is only for experts.

In such markets you should never act without a safety net.

DU9629965S

96

Use your subscription right to purchase additional inexpensive shares of a successful public limited company when it carries out a capital increase.

97

Your money is only as safe as the bank that you have trusted with it. Inform yourself whether and to what amount savings deposits are covered.

98

Don't give away your money
to the government—fill in your tax forms every year!
Many people will be surprised to find
they are entitled to a rebate.

99

If the promised or allegedly guaranteed return

on an investment is more than 70%

it is either a speculative investment or you are looking at a fraud.

100

HV 22.04.1998

The economist Franco Modigliani received the 1985 Nobel prize for his concept of life cycles as the secret to optimal financial planning. According to his theory, your expenses and investment decisions should be adapted to suit your phase of life in order to manage your money successfully.

Hoch
08.11.1S
86.0
Tief
10.07.1S
11.6
Tolera
637.73
Vol(2E
56.64
Gewir
Verlu
BarD
-1.0
CashF

S:04.0
0.51

Kurs: 86.00

1994   1995   1996   1997   1998   1999   2 (c) Tai

2083 Kurse   08.11.1999

Tai-Pan (c) 1995 Lenz + Partner GmbH

The eternal question about how the economy and the stock market will develop can be answered clearly. In the long run they will always be up. The economy, i.e., businesses, are simply the motor of the world, and it will continue running. Parts have to be exchanged once in a while, though, meaning that markets change.

101

102

Over the last 24 years, the Dow Jones has, on average, doubled every 6.5 years. Thus the question of when a share is overpriced can be answered easily. Before a correction relatively many shares are overprice; after a correction only a few.

103

Sell successful investments before your profits dwindle again.

Even with fixed-term deposits and other investments, the tougher you negotiate the more interest you will get!

104

105

Use your higher interest savings
account or day-to-day account only
as a place to accumulate money! As
soon as you have saved 300 £ or
more, transfer it to another form of
investment that will offer a larger
return in the long run.

106

If you absolutely cannot part with a savings account, at least look for one that offers a high interest rate and credits accrued interest at least quarterly, so that after taking into account inflation and taxes your money doesn't actually decrease.

ternationale Aktien

107

The better informed you are about current interest rates, economic trends and the political environment, the better your bank will treat you in conversations.

	19.06.00	16.06.00
o Nobel	42.00	1.50G
ba	32.00	32.00G
azon.com	46.30G	49.00b
erican Express	55.50-T	56.00G
gen	70.50B	70.50b
	56.30G	56.50b
le Comp.	96.00G	93.80bB
T	35.50G	36.00b
Atlantic Ffm	60.00-T	59.00T
South Ffm	49.00-T	50.00T
Amoco	9.70G	9.50G
eing	40.50G	42.00b
ish Airways	5.80G	5.80G
	10.00G	10.00G
ion	47.40G	47.00b
erpillar	37.00G	39.50G
co Systems	70.00G	69.01b

Biotest St.Fr
BMW Vz.
Co.Bau&Bd.#
Condomi#
CompuGrou
DAB#
Debitel #
Dolerit Basal
Dom-Brauer
Dt. Bet.#
Dt. Steinz. F
Didier
Dyckerh. St.
Eifelhöhenkli
Eisenhüttenw
Eurobike**
Eurohypo**
F + G#
Ford Werke*
Gerling Allg.

108

Caution is advised when it comes to tax saving plans!

An investment that is not profitable before taxes

most often does not reach a noticeable revenue after taxes, either.

109

If you are inclined to buy a product upon the recommendation of a friend without knowing its name or whether it is a share, a warrant, or other security, it is better to leave it alone.

110

Stock market experts look not only at the fundamental data of an enterprise, but also take the chart analysis into account when making decisions.

111

The price earnings ratio (PER) of a company is not the only factor
to consider when you want to purchase shares.
The technology stock exchange in the United States,
for instance, offers an average PER of just 180 to 250,
but remains interesting.

112

Growth stocks usually have a higher PER than cyclical shares. This is due to their nature, because growth stocks reinvest all their profits in order to continue their perpetual expansion. They rarely yield a dividend.

113

Are you a typical day trader?!

Hopefully, you are among the winners.

According to American studies,

80% of all day traders fail to succeed in the long run.

114

Teach your children to deal with money, correctly and
with goals in mind, as early as possible.
Help them be among the youngest millionaires!

115

Incidents like the demise of Barings Bank demonstrate that banks are not always secure, and that in the worst case many of their customers can lose much of their personal fortunes. It is imperative to know the extent to which your money is insured, for example through the deposit guaranty fund.

116

Negotiate your interest rate, or change over
to a bank that offers you more.

117

Keep the balance in your savings account as low as possible.
The standard amount set aside for emergencies is approximately
two to three months' salary—but it can be better stashed than in a
savings account.

118

In a period of high interest rates, don't forget to shift your fixed-term deposit investment, for example into fixed-interest securities that you can access at any time and offer you a higher yield.

119

When you extend fixed-term deposit investments
beyond the initially agreed upon date of maturity,
have the accrued interest added to your initial investment
rather than deposited in your giro account—otherwise you will
miss out on the compound interest effect.

120

With shares and equity funds, risk diversification is the
alpha and omega of a successful investment.

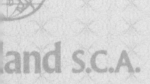

121

You can be successful with shares only if you as a rule distribute your money in several shares and sectors.

122

Avoid entering the stock market if the inflation rate has risen sharply in the previous 12 to 24 months!

123

Take the effort to compile an assets and liability statement
each year. It is the only means to find out whether your prior
investments truly performed as you had hoped, taking into account
both revenue and taxation, or whether you need to make changes
in order to reach your goals.

124

Location and quality are always key factors for the increase in value of real estate. Keep this in mind when buying.

125

The lower purchasing fees offered by discount brokers
also mean doing without extensive advisory service.
At the end of the day, this can be very expensive.

126

The success of an investment in index-linked bonds
clearly depends on the price/performance relationship
as well as the price risk it entails.

127

There is more than one way of doing things!

But on the other hand,

any given consultant will not necessarily

have the perfect investment for you.

Make sure you have consultants you trust and are comfortable with.

128

Buy shares low and sell high,
and not vice versa!
Simple, isn't it?

129

You can consider yourself wealthy when have enough capital
to live off its proceeds.

130

Whether you become rich is primarily a question of your inner convictions and the people with whom you surround yourself!

131

Question:

How do I make a small fortune at the stock exchange?

Answer:

By investing a large fortune badly!

132

The annual rate of return is the profit gained in relation to the capital invested, expressed as a percentage. However, it does not tell you anything if you haven't taken into account inflation, cost, price gains or losses, and possible taxes.

133

With fixed-interest securities,
the net yield—rather than a high
interest rate—is crucial for the success of
your investment.

134

The interest rate situation and time remaining to maturity influence the price of a fixed-interest security. The longer the remaining life, the more strongly the price reacts to changes in the current market interest rate.

135

Convertible bonds are ideal
if you want to become a shareholder by exchanging the bond into
shares after a rise in market price.

136

You can realise high stock price gains with convertible bonds when the stock market is booming.

137

Use stock exchange and investors' seminars to increase your knowledge. Every pound invested in registration fees will be returned doubly to tenfold by better investment results later on!

138

The earlier you begin saving,
the smaller the amount you must save
monthly to reach the same goal.

139

Frugality, and not a high income,
is still the surest way to prosperity
and wealth.

140

Be sure to inquire and inform yourself about low-interest

government loans or other special programs.

141

You don't have to buy foreign shares in foreign countries.
In fact, it is usually less expensive to buy them
at a local stock market.

142

Beware! People who have recently acquired money tend to spend every last pound.

Real millionaires always contemplate how they can increase their money still further, and do not throw it out the window.

143

Before investing in schemes to save on taxes, consider thoroughly whether you would buy the object even if it were offered for your net capital investment. In other words, you have to consider whether the object is worth its after-tax price. Always think about the economic background before deciding to buy.

144

Money market funds are an ideal short-term investment because of their short time to maturity, the low price risk, and the market-oriented interest rate.

145

Foreign government securities are an interesting investment
not only because of their attractive interest rates,
but also because of possible currency gains.

146

What is the difference between an old man
and an elderly gentleman?

Very simple: Nothing but the money he has at his disposal.

147

Dormant equity holdings promise a high return on investment, but take care, as these holdings often go nowhere. Stated clearly, after filling the hands of others, you may be left empty handed.

148

Smoking may keep you slim, but certainly not rich. Spare
yourself the smoke and invest the money profitably!
Only one pack a day less can save you 50 £ each month.
If you were to invest this money for 30 years,
you could have accumulated approximately 200,000 £.
(Source: Templeton Growth Fd. March 1970 to March 2000)
Not only are you likely to live longer, you can also live better.
So stop smoking.

106835D7

149

When the stock market is unstable, convertible bonds are an ideal form of investment because they offer a modest but guaranteed rate of interest.
Upon recovery of the stock market, there are good prospects for stock price gains with a limited price risk.

150

When share prices fall, hopes for a fast reversal of the trend are seldom fulfilled. It is better to sell in good time and then reinvest as soon as a turnaround is in sight, while prices are still low.

KD 3 1 0 6 8 3 5 D 7

151

An annual assets and liabilities assessment shows you whether you have found an asset mix that fits your expectations and mentality, or whether you need to fine-tune your strategy.

152

The best investment strategy for shares is:

"Buy when there's bad news and sell when there's good news!"

153

Between ages 50 and 60 is your last opportunity
to correct your previous mistakes
in order to enjoy a generous supplementary income
and avoid having to spend your retirement
dependent solely on a goverment pension.

154

In financing real estate, there is an ever stronger trend toward using unit trusts to significantly reduce the payback period and thus the total cost of the property.

155

There are myriad unit trusts, in countless variations.

You can certainly find one suitable for just about any purpose!

156

Performance comparisons as a basis for choosing a fund
are only one indicator. Your investment goal,
the duration of your investment, and
your willingness to take risks are equally important factors.

157

Individual investments in Eastern Europe are still very risky. Instead, invest in participating shares in the Middle and Eastern European index funds.

158

The differences among index certificates are great.
Get full information about risks, opportunities and costs before
buying them. And remember, the spoken word is soon forgotten—
be sure to get all pertinent information in writing.

159

Open real estate funds are no replacement
for your own real estate.

160

Mixed funds are not necessarily a top notch
investment—only a few actively managed funds
offer genuinely attractive results. So keep your
eyes open when selecting one!

HV:22.04.1998

161

Negotiate with your bank about fees, or use discount brokers and direct banks.

162

Shares are very well suited to speculation, especially newly issued shares. But not every issue will yield the expected profit. Negative developments and shares that do not budge are not unusual.

163

There are two ways to get rich:
Either you lower your expenses and expectations,
or you increase your financial means by targeted
money multiplication!

164

Never sell shares when the market is falling if you do not absolutely
have to. Instead, act anti-cyclically and use the opportunity
to buy or stock up on shares.

165

Don't be overly impressed by seemingly inexpensive offers from
direct brokers. Performance is more important than fees!

If you adhere to the following rule, you can consider yourself an investment professional and have made the right investment decision: In low interest phases with interest rates tending to rise, invest only in fixed-interest securities with a short remaining life. In high interest phases with interest rates tending to fall, invest in long-term high interest securities.

167

Beware of closed-end real estate funds!
They will tie up your capital and make it nearly inaccessible
for as long as 20 to 25 years.

168

Whether you pay 30 £ or 1 million £ per month into a fund, there is no other form of investment that offers you such a wide range of opportunities and choices.

No matter what your investment goal or chosen duration of investment, funds can be a good possibility.

169

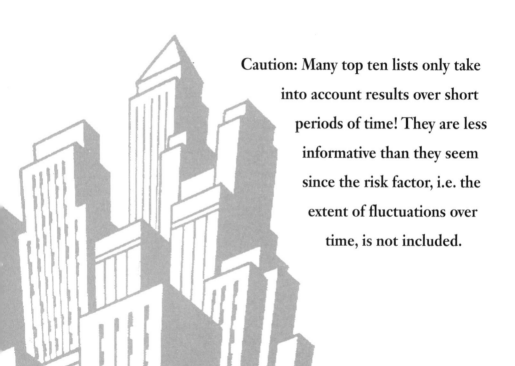

Caution: Many top ten lists only take
into account results over short
periods of time! They are less
informative than they seem
since the risk factor, i.e. the
extent of fluctuations over
time, is not included.

Shares and funds belong in every deposit!
Studies have shown that between 1918 and 1992,
shares yielded an annual profit of 11.9%
and bonds 5.7% in England.
If you take into account inflation, the yield of shares
was 7.3% annually, while bonds yielded a paltry 1.1%.

170

Since smaller and direct banks do not maintain a network of branch offices, they have lower costs than traditional banks. They are tendentially more cautious about approving loans, but usually offer a higher interest rate than the larger banks.

171

Money market funds are an attractive alternative to
savings accounts. They offer fast access and relatively
low risk—and you can start with as little as
35 £ per month!

173

Investing in precious metals, especially gold,
was considered an important part of any depository in the past.
Since gold has lost in importance as the safeguard of currencies,
it will not be possible to make spectacular profits with gold
in the near future.

174

The success of asset allocation
is strongly dependent on a wide diversification
and less dependent on timing.

175

Fund of funds are the ideal investment form if you want
an investment that requires little maintenance
but at the same time offers a wide distribution
into a huge variety of funds.
In the best case, they gather a selection of the best funds
worldwide, all under one roof!

176

Various economic studies have shown that a selection of 10 to 15 titles guarantees a sufficient distribution of risk in most international stock markets.

177

Funds with a high price fluctuation,
such as sector, country or regional funds,
are especially suitable for saving plans.

178

Greed gone awry: If you look into the mirror and see large pound signs in your eyes, take a step back from your planned investment.

179

The price earning ratio (PER) measures the earning power
or the internal value of a company,
and indicates whether the company's shares are
attractive or overpriced.
However, the price earning ratio is no guarantee
for the success of your investment.

180

The best funds are not necessarily those with a large volume,

but more often the smaller ones!

181

The high flying funds of the past are not necessarily
the stars of the future. Keep an eye on continuity!

182

For speculators and investors with strong nerves, funds from the
tiger states can be extremely profitable!

183

If you distribute your funds according to your investment goals
and the life span of each investment,
you will be in a good position to react to every possible situation.

184

The higher the promised yield of a share,
the higher the risks you bear.

GD(200): 48.19

| LOG | 1 1992 | 1993 | 1994 | 1995 |

T:15.10.98 14.11.1991 208

185

If you have to pay taxes on interest or dividends, your return after taxes is more important than a high dividend or interest!

Tief
10.07.1997
11.66

Toleranz
637.73%

Vol(250)
56.64%

Gewinn
Verlust

BarDiv
-1.00

CashFlow

S:04.01.99
0.5113

Kurs: 86.00

1997   1998   1999   2
08.11.1999

(c) Tai-Pan

186

Be cautious with telephone salespeople. Especially when charismatic salespeople promise a great return with futures trading and private placements on the phone, you can expect a total financial loss in the short or long run in most cases.

Don't let a stock market boom
tempt you to invest too large a portion
of your assets in high risk investments.

187

There is no one analytical
process that will yield the
sole profitable solution.
Always rely on your gut feelings.

188

189

Key figures are comparisons that help analysts
and private investors determine the relative attractiveness
of individual shares in relation to the sector and the overall market.

190

The development of wind as a source of energy is and will remain a high-risk investment, suitable only for investors with a lot of courage and a high tax bracket.

Derivatives are suitable only for born gamblers, who even in
roulette use no strategy and bet on
either red or black.

191

Options and futures are complex forms of investment, and are best left to expert stock market professionals.

192

193

Investing in equity funds is more comfortable than buying individual shares.

194

Funds are the simplest way of
administrating your money profitably.

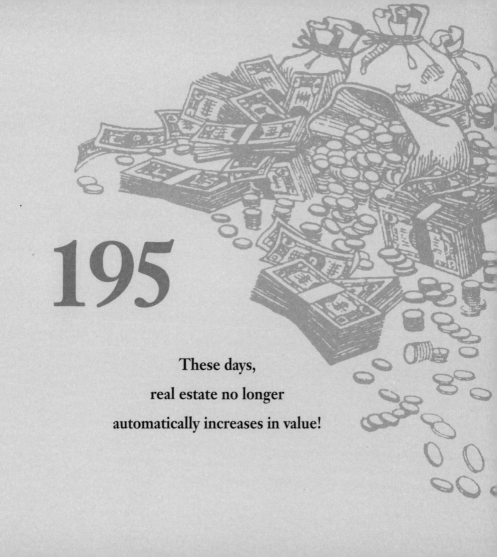

195

These days,
real estate no longer
automatically increases in value!

196

Choose only high interest investments when buying fixed-interest securities, as long as their price is low.

197

You will attain optimal results with fixed-interest securities

only if you are willing to continually

inform yourself about interest rate trends

and adjust your investment accordingly.

198

You can increase the profit of your fund investments by having any potential dividends reinvested, preferably automatically, without additional costs. These are called cumulative funds.

199

Open real estate funds are not an adequate replacement for real estate.

200

Flexibility pays off with any investment.

201

You will be amazed to see the amount you can accumulate over several years of relatively low—but regular—payments into unit trusts through the cost-average effect.

202

Speculating on tax-free increases in the price of fixed-interest securities always pays off.

The key factor for your success is the right timing!

203

Bonds with a remaining life span of 10 years and longer should be bought only when interest rates are high, never when they are low.

204

You can only see the return on your
investment after you have deducted
fees and bank charges!

205

If you want to sleep well, buy bonds.
If you want to eat well, buy shares.
John D. Rockefeller

206

Funds are not suitable for long-term investments.

207

The higher the earning possibilities of a fund,
the greater the price fluctuations and the risk of losses.

208

Fund picking is usually a more expensive form of fund administration. Its success is largely dependent on the conditions, fees and the correct choice of funds. Inform yourself in detail before investing.

209

If speciality or sector funds alone are too speculative for you,
choose a fund of funds that contains only these kinds of funds.
You will have a great profit with a limited price risk!

210

The decisive factor for the success of your investment

is not a high interest rate,

but what remains in your purse after you subtract

taxes, fees and possible losses.

211

It is not the recommendations of banks or stock market "gurus"
that will help you make a profit on the stock exchange.
Your own knowledge, opinions, and decisions
are the key factors in your success.

212

Through cost averaging, you can usually acquire shares
at a lower average price than if you invest the sum all in one go.
This is especially applicable in markets
that fluctuate strongly.

213

Never invest funds financed by loans
in the stock market!
Major financial crises have been triggered this way.

Always take both price and value into
account when purchasing real estate.
Not all that glitters is stable in value.
Location, location, location—
and structural integrity, all combined
with a fair price—are the key factors for
sustainable increase in value.

214

215

To learn how to make more out of your
money, you need to talk with experts and
not lay people or sales representatives who
are motivated by their own profit.

216

The danger of derivatives lies in the fact that your betting partners are banks, and they always win, at least with the fees they charge, and even more if your assessments are mistaken.

217

If you have a limited knowledge of the capital market,

stay clear of derivatives!

These transactions are not profitable

for the investor 70% of the time.

218

Investment companies usually offer in-house depositories that are less expensive than bank depositories, or even completely free of charge.

219

Fund savings plans are an ideal way to accumulate capital. You need not commit yourself to fixed payment amounts and times as with insurances, and your money remains readily accessible; the amount and timing of your savings can be chosen freely.

220

The higher the volatility of a share,
the more valuable its warrant.

Stock market pros buy only undervalued warrants because these turn a higher profit than shares—and the profit is achieved much faster!

221

REGISTERED

NUMBER

U 1182

KERR-M^CGEI

8½% SINKING FUND

222 *Kerr = Mc Gee Corpora*

Date of Delaware, therein referre

8½%

JUNE 1,
2006

50000 U   1182

*CCC0093

Invest in new offerings only if you enjoy taking risks!

**FIFTY T

or registered assigns,the principal sum of

on June 1, 2006, and to pay interest thereon from June 1, 1976, or from the most recent interest Payment Date to which interest has
of twelve 30-day months), until the principal hereof is paid or duly provided for. The interest so payable, and punctually paid or duly pr
(or one or more Predecessor Debentures, as defined in such Indenture) is registered at the close of business on the Regular Record Date
Any such interest not so punctually paid or duly provided for shall forthwith cease to be payable to the Holder on such Regular Reco
Special Record Date for the payment of such Defaulted Interest to be fixed by the Trustee, notice whereof shall be given to Holders
ments of any securities exchange on which the Debentures may be listed, and upon such notice as may be required by such excha
agency of the Company maintained for that purpose in the Borough of Manhattan, The City of New York, In such coin or currency
interest may be made at the option of the Company by check mailed to the address of the Person entitled thereto as such address

223

Trading funds are not automatically better
than funds with offering premiums.
Only the long-term results will show the difference.

ORPORATION

RE DUE JUNE 1, 2006

oration duly organized and existing
Company), for value received, hereby promises to pay to

CO

SEE REVERSE FOR
CERTAIN DEFINITIONS

CUSIP 492386 AC 1

DOLLARS

vided for, semi-annually on June 1 and December 1 in each year, at the rate of 8½% per annum (computed on the basis of x year
terest Payment Date or within 30 days thereafter will, as provided in such Indenture, be paid to the Person in whose name this Debenture
shall be the May 15 or November 15 (whether or not a Business Day), as the case may be, next preceding such Interest Payment Date.
held to the Person in whose name this Debenture (or one or more Predecessor Debentures) is registered at the close of business on a
than 10 days prior to such Special Record Date, or may be paid at any time in any other lawful manner not inconsistent with the require-
vided in such Indenture. Payment of the principal of (and premium, if any) and interest on this Debenture will be made at the office or
of America as at the time of payment is legal tender for payment of public and private debts; provided, however, that payment of
re Register.

224

Recognise trends before others do!
As soon as you read a recommendation in the
financial newspapers, it is most often already too late.

225

With derivatives, you are speculating purely on the future, and hope to earn a lot of money if your assessment is correct.

226

Treat top-ten fund lists with caution!
Every analyst calculates differently, and five comparisons
generally yield five different results!

227

Does it make you nervous if shares that acquired four weeks ago are still in the minus? If so, stay away from speculation. The stock exchange is the wrong playground for you!

228

Even with shares that have
demonstrated a steady increase over
the last 30 years, such as
McDonalds, you must take into
account the possibility of slumps up
to 40%. Such are the ways of the
stock exchange!

229

Power is found in tranquility.

Give the stock exchange some time to regain strength.

In the past, downwards trends have seldom continued

for more than 6 months.

Real estate is often offered at
a test price—always assume that
the price is negotiable.
With a little negotiation finesse, you
can save a lot of money.

230

231

Regardless of the period, evaluation of a fund's performance offers only limited orientation because it can only evaluate the past.

232

Important is not only the performance of a fund, but also the risks taken by fund management in order to achieve this result.

233

With the help of money market
funds you can change foreign
currencies into Euro at any time
and pay little or no fees,
or you can park foreign currencies
in money market funds with
higher interest rates.

234

With funds as with other products, there shouldn't be incongruity between labeling and content—i.e., if the fund sells itself as environmentally friendly or ethical, it had better be environmentally friendly or ethical! Read the fund brochure and the current report.

235

You should be interested in shares with high dividends only if you can receive these dividends primarily without taxation!

236

Whether your stock investment becomes successful or not
is always a question of the price at which you bought
and continuing favourable development of those stocks.

237

Investing in warrants is profitable
only if the market climate is favourable, the warrant is evaluated
positively and, of course, if the timing is right!

238

If you cannot decide whether to invest in shares or in bonds, invest in convertible bonds.

239

If you do not want to exercise your stock option,
you can sell it profitably at the stock exchange.

HV:22.04.1998

240

The stock exchange deals in the future,
not in the present.

241

If you are a security conscious investor, invest only in Triple-A funds. They invest primarily in government bond issues or securities guaranteed by the governments of the leading developed countries and in first class industrial corporations.

242

Junk bonds are for speculative investors only.

They offer above-average profit opportunities with a high risk,

although the risk is limited through broad diversification.

243

Never forget to sell in due time.

Only then you have actually made a profit with your investment.

244

Active trading is necessary with shares.

It is not sufficient to invest once

and then look where your share price is after 5 years.

Not many shares have a steady increase.

245

Always invest in new trends, never in old ones!

246

The stock exchange is like a lift:
It isn't dangerous to go to the basement.
Just keep your nerves, and it will go up again.

247

Decisive for a certain profit from high interest securities
is not the interest rate, but the credit rating of the issuer!

248

Always take inflation into account
when calculating the annual rate of return of your investment.

249

Refrain from investing in long-term bonds
when interest rates are rising—losses in price are guaranteed.

250

Nowadays, it is not terribly profitable to acquire gold
in the form of gold coins.
The prospects for a rising gold price
will only improve when inflation rises sharply globally
and most of the central banks have reduced their gold reserves
by selling them.

251

If you have gold coins,
keep them. Better times
will come!

252

Diamonds are a great investment
when it comes to jewellery but not
when it comes to profit!

253

The tremendous number of offerings by various insurance companies make it a confusing area.

Treat yourself to a neutral consultant before signing an insurance contract! The fee that you pay for her or his services is much less expensive than insurance that costs too much.

254

Life insurance, even unit-linked life insurance, is not always suitable for providing for your old age.

The costs are high and the return is simply too low.

255

If you do buy life insurance, be sure to search out a company that has reasonable prices and can demonstrate long-term results.

256

If you have between
300 £ and 1500 £,
treasury bonds are the
right choice for a
1- or 2-year investment!

Forget the standard recommendations
of your consultant or your bank. You can only
achieve results with investments that are
customised to your tax and personal situation,
your personal investment goals, and your
financial possibilities.

257

258

Zero bonds were formerly very popular,

but they have lost their attractiveness

because they react strongly to every change in interest rates.

If the interest rate in the capital market rises,

the prices plunge in a free fall.

This is why they are not currently a recommendable investment.

259

Floaters offer continuous high yields in times of rising interest (as is currently the case) because the interest on these fixed-interest bonds is adapted quarterly to the market interest rate, making the price risk is very small.

260

The well-known proverb
"good things take time"
applies to practically every investment transaction.

261

The daily market prices for shares already contain
the expectations for the next few days.

262

When central banks raise interest rates substantially, it most often leads to a decline in prices or a slowdown in the stock exchange. This can influence your balance sheet profits immensely.

263

The success of your equity fund investment is largely dependent
on the duration of the investment and the strategy of the funds.
Only international and highly diversified funds
are suitable as a basic investment.

REGISTERED

NUMBER

U 1182

264

KERR-McGEE

8½% SINKING FUND

Kerr - McGee Corporation
under the laws of the State of Delaware, therein referred

High yield bonds are the most interesting fixed-interest securities.

8½%
JUNE 1,
2006

＊ ＊CCC0093

＊＊FIFTY T

or registered assigns,the principal sum of

on June 1, 2006, and to pay interest thereon from June 1, 1976, or from the most recent Interest Payment Date to which interest has be of twelve 30-day months), until the principal hereof is paid or duly provided for. The interest so payable, and punctually paid or duly pro (or one or more Predecessor Debentures, as defined in such Indenture) is registered at the close of business on the Regular Record Date Any such interest not so punctually paid or duly provided for shall forthwith cease to be payable to the Holder on such Regular Record Special Record Date for the payment of such Defaulted Interest to be fixed by the Trustee, notice whereof shall be given to Holders of ments of any securities exchange on which the Debentures may be listed, and upon such notice as may be required by such exchange; agency of the Company maintained for that purpose in the Borough of Manhattan, The City of New York, in such coin or currency interest may be made at the option of the Company by check mailed to the address of the Person entitled thereto at such address sho Reference is hereby made to the further provisions of this Debenture set forth on the reverse hereof, which further provisions s Unless the certificate of authentication hereon has been executed by or on behalf of the Trustee referred to on the reverse h

RPORATION

265

_E_ DUE JUNE 1, 2006

oration duly organized and existing
Company), for value received, hereby promises to pay to

Fixed-interest securities usually offer a better return on investment
than fixed-term deposits, and you can sell them at any time.

DOLLARS

266

Trend funds are "in" —
and achieve great results with a calculable risk.

267

The price risk of fixed-interest securities is mirrored in annuity funds. Keep an eye on the current interest rate situation before entering to protect yourself from unpleasant surprises.

268

When selecting volatile funds, see to it that movement between

funds within the investment company is free

and possible at any time.

This makes trading easier and increases your return.

269

Due to the cost average effect, you may achieve dream returns with saving plans in speciality funds!

270

Do not make buying or selling decisions according to individual analyses alone. Before you have finished reading all of them, they will be outdated.

271

Have you found great tips and buying signals in newspapers, stock exchange publications or other media?
These are already old hat! By the time the media reports the "news", the market has already digested it.

272

Never forget that the stock exchange is faster than radio, television or the print media. The stock exchange in New York, for example, integrates company information into share prices within 6 seconds. Europe requires a full 30 seconds to react.

273

Think about the way you order:

Shares can be ordered fastest online, via the Internet from direct banks. By comparison, banks and smaller branches can take up to 1 1/2 days to process your order.

274

Never wager your house and home!
Investments on credit can endanger
your livelihood if your speculation is
not successful.

275

Time and information are the
foundations of a successful investment.

276

Practice discipline. Thoughtless
decisions often lead to chaos.

277

Money market funds can be an attractive alternative to the usual investments for saving. Especially in times of rising interest rates, they are a profitable investment instrument.

278

If you invest the major part of your assets well,

the smaller part cannot do much damage.

On the other hand, if you have invested 95% of your assets

unprofitably, the damage cannot be undone with the remaining 5%.

279

Use fixed-term deposits as a temporary way station,
but never as a long-term investment.

280

A stock market crash always brings with it
an opportunity for a new beginning.
Investors oriented toward long-term investments should use it.

281

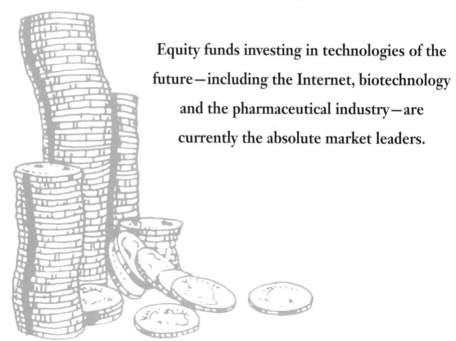

Equity funds investing in technologies of the
future—including the Internet, biotechnology
and the pharmaceutical industry—are
currently the absolute market leaders.

282

Don't underestimate the currency risk

when investing in foreign securities!

Great profits are often depleted by currency fluctuations.

283

If you have already bought capital sum life insurance or private annuity insurance and are upset about the low return on your investment, you now have the possibility to optimise it.

If the cash surrender value of your insurance policy amounts to at least 16,000 £, you can borrow 1.6-fold that amount, giving you 26,000 £ to invest in the best international funds at a renowned Swiss bank in order to reach optimal returns.

284

Stock market crises can be anticipated—

real crashes cannot!

Dow Chemical	36.00-T	36.66-T	Herlitz St.#
DSM	34.30G	34.80G	Herlitz Vz.#
Du Pont	48.00G	48.50b	Hirsch#
Eastman Kodak	61.50G	62.00B	Indus Hold.
Elsevier	12.40G	12.00b	Interseroh*
Ericsson	21.50G	22.70G	
Exxon Mobil			Kolber M
Fiat	29.00G	27.00G	
Ford Motor	46.50G	47.00G	Abit#
General Electric	52.50G	55.00b	Advast#
General Motors	66.00G	70.00b	Aixtron#
Glaxo Wellcome	28.50G	28.50G	Artnet.com
Heineken	59.00G	59.50G	Antwerpes
Hewlett Packard	120.00xD	121.00b	Augusta T
Home Depot	51.00G	52.00G	Baldat#
Honda Motor	34.50G	33.80G	Basler#
Honeywell	44.00B	53.00G	BB Biotech
HSBC Hold. Ffm	12.00G	12.15G	Bertrandt#
3M	119.50G	122.00b	BinTec Co
Intel Corp.	136.50G	135.00b	Biodata Inf

285

Before investing your money, consider very precisely which of your
financial goals you wish to achieve with that acquisition.

	11.00G	11.00G	Weru Ffm	2.
	10.50B	10.50G	WMF Vz.#	0.64	1:
	21.20G	21.00G	Zanders St.	6:
0.92	28.30G	28.00G	Zanders Vz.	5
0.36	11.00G		ürich R.I.*	10.23	2

Only if you are familiar with and compare the offers of several banks will you be able to select the one that best suits you.

Ffm			Neuer Markt Ffm	1
	33.60G	31.20G	IXOS Software#	2(
	585.00b	598.00b	Jack White#	2:
0.09	143.00b	148.00b	Jumptec#	1(
	8.00b	8.50b	Kabel New Media#	2:
	18.00b	18.40b	Kinowelt***	6:
1.02	99.50b	99.50b	LHS Group**	3!
	45.15b	44.00b	Lintec#	1
	73.00b	72.70b	MB Software#	1
	101.80b	99.90b	Medion#	1.48	1:
0.27	14.50b	15.00b	Micrologica#	1
	28.00b	26.50b	Mobilcom#	0.25	1
	360.00b	358.00b	MWG Biotech#	1
	14.00b	14.05b	Nemetschek#	

Due to their higher management fees, funds without offering premiums, so-called trading funds, are profitable only when their results are genuinely good and you deal with them intelligently.

287

288

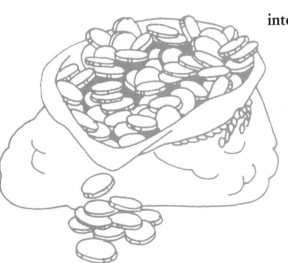

A withdrawal plan from international equity funds— that is, an investment pension—is the best retirement pension plan!

289

Don't make the mistake of betting all your assets on one horse.
Your chances of losing everything are far greater
than the chances that you will earn money with it.

As a rule, independent professional consultants are worth more than their fees! In the jungle of possible investments, they can help you find the object that is just right for you.

290

291

International security funds make use of internationally offered high interest bonds. The risk of currency fluctuation is greatly reduced by diversification into various currencies, leading to remarkable returns on investment.

292

Fixed-interest securities are only
as profit yielding and as secure as the credit
standing of the debtor,
so keep an eye on the ratings.

293

Do not sign bonus, premium,
or multiple interest savings agreements!
These benefit only the bank.
Fund savings agreements are a much better bet.

294

Negotiate conditions!

This is the first commandment of getting better offers and

achieving higher earnings.

295

Fixed-term deposits or London interest rate investments
are ideal in times of rising interest rates.

296

Invest your money in international markets that are expected
to experience strong economic growth.

297

Save 2 £ daily, and you will have 60 £ a month that you can invest profitably in good equity funds.

298

Stay clear of investment companies that demand
high switching fees. This makes switching funds difficult.

GD(200): 48.19

HV:22.04.1998

299

You can further increase your earnings with equity funds
by paying into them regularly as with a savings plan.
The so-called cost-average effect ensures your profit
even when prices are falling.

10.07.1997
11.66
Toleranz
637.73%
Vol(250)
56.64%
Gewinn
Verlust
BarDiv
-1.00
CashFlow

S:04.01.99
Kurs: 86.00   0.5113
1997   1998   1999   2 (c) Tai-Pan

300

Avoiding losses is the key to success in every investment!

301

Diversify your investment by buying shares of at least
10 different companies.
If that is beyond your means, invest in
equity funds.

302

If you invest in the very best equity funds, you don't have to look after anything and can achieve great returns over a long period.

303

Young companies, so-called "small caps", often offer better possibilities for earning money than blue chip companies. Make the most of these possibilities!

304

Increasing the number of shares or your stake in an equity fund you have already invested in is profitable only if they have good prospects.

305

If you cannot invest a lot of time and money, funds are a better alternative than shares.

306

Should your shares or your fund decline more than average, ask your advisor for the reasons in order to have the option of selling with limited losses.

307

Before investing in shares or funds, look at the chart development to be sure that you are not buying at a peak.

308

An ideal mixture of your portfolio
includes investments not only in stocks from your own country,
but also in American and other foreign funds.

309

The most reliable barometer for
foreign stock exchanges is the Dow Jones.
Its ups and downs are seen as indicators of the
probability for gains or losses in shares.
Watch such trends.

310

If you want to make money with shares, you must know the ins and out of the stock exchange—otherwise you will become hopelessly lost.

311

Don't buy just because it's fashionable to invest in new markets. At least find out what exactly you are buying.

312

Subscribing to new issues is very popular, the demand high, and profits seem guaranteed. However, with many new issues the sobering news come right after the stock market debut.

313

Keep in mind:
When banks advertise
shares, it is not the
investor that is at the
centre of attention.

314

Equity funds, no matter how diversified, are subject to price risks. Therefore, you should never invest your total resources in equity funds.

315

In order to prevent unpleasant surprises,
you must inform yourself about the investment strategy
and the risks involved in an equity fund before you invest in it.

316

To make a profit from speciality, sector, or theme funds, you must pay constant attention to current developments at the stock exchange and fast-paced fund developments.

317

High yield funds are an interesting investment if you are looking for a mixture of high interest bonds without the risk of an individual purchase.

318

Before purchasing shares, successful investors consider the so-called beta factor, which helps you assess the sensitivity of the desired share to fluctuations in the overall market.

319

If you are expecting a rising market,

invest in shares with a high beta factor,

because these promise above average price gains.

320

In times of insecurity on the stock market,
shares with a low beta factor are more interesting
because they don't participate fully in every price decline.

321

Great gains at the stock exchange are only yours to keep
if you actually sell your shares!

322

The secret of a successful investment strategy
is not to miss the most advantageous time to sell or buy!
That is all.

323

If you do not pay attention to your bonds, you will lose
a few percentage points of return on investment.
If you do not pay attention to your shares,
you may lose everything.

324

Avoid the "trends are your friend" attitude of typical investors.
Don't jump on a moving train—it could change directions on you.

325

Don't chase profits. If you have missed the right time
to buy, wait for a price correction later on,
or look for another share to acquire.

326

Never invest all your money at one time.
Keep a small sum available so that you can buy
in case of a price slump.

327

Set a price goal that you want to reach with your shares, and sell when it is attained.

328

The stock exchange always recovers after a slump.

Learn to sit out the slumps,

and never sell when the prices have hit bottom.

329

One distinguishes between value shares and growth shares.

Currently, more money can be made with growth shares.

330

In a time when interest rates are high but tending to decline, long-term investments not only give you a high interest gain, but also a nice (and in some circumstances tax-free) profit upon selling.

331

In a time when interest rates are low but tending to rise, fixed-interest securities offer little revenue. Shares or funds should be your favourites in this situation.

332

You can afford speculative shares only if you have the time to follow up on these investments frequently and regularly.

333

Keep your hands off of great offers made over the phone!
They are more likely to be a way to get rid of your money fast.

334

Examine your daily spending behaviour.
You will be surprised to see exactly where and how you spend
your money, and how much you can save if you consider
each and every purchase!

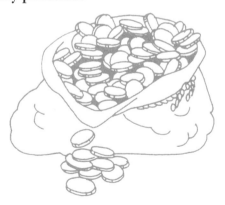

335

Depending on your tax situation, high dividends may or may not be interesting from a tax perspective — long-term growth and price gains, however, are always to your advantage.

336

Even the safest fixed-interest securities
contain an unavoidable price risk.
The risk does not go away
if you put your head in the sand!
Philip L. Carret

337

If you want to know exactly how a fund invests
the money entrusted to it, and whether it can be profitable,
you must read the sales information and the last annual report.

338

Only warrants that are traded regularly and in sufficient number offer an optimal protection against losses.

339

If you know and don't act, you didn't know!

340

Caution: With red-hot stock exchange tips,
the only one who usually benefits is the publisher!

341

Don't let greed go to your head.

Stay reasonable, and be content with realistic profits!

342

The profitability of a warrant can
be seen in its leverage.

343

Warrants are hot speculations—the opportunities and risks are far
greater than with a share. Don't get burned!

344

If you are looking for the advantages of a fixed-interest security
with simultaneous profit from price gains at the stock exchange,
you should invest in convertible debenture stock.

345

Only if you buy and sell
at the appropriate times can you make
a profit at the stock exchange.

346

For every buyer there must be a seller—
otherwise you have no deal.

347

Don't bet on exotic shares. This market is very slim,
and in the worst case you may get stuck with your shares because
no one wants to buy them.

348

In order to be able to speculate
successfully, you need capital,
courage, and good judgement!

Philip L. Carret

349

The potential for losses in your share deposits and funds
can be limited only with puts on the respective market index,
and then only when your deposit or fund
is very similar to the respective index.

350

The cheapest way to safeguard your existing deposit against losses is to sell the account.

351

To and fro—your money will go.

Don't trade too much, and do exercise patience.

Some shares need time.

Better a loss of shares with short-term discomfort

than a long-term disaster with constant losses.

353

Bad timing can seldom be corrected by simply waiting it out!

354

A broad mix of sectors brings constancy to your deposit,
and you avoid large plunges in the value
of your deposit if one sector slumps.

355

The smaller your deposit, the larger your risk with single shares.

356

The statement "shares beat bonds" is valid only for deposits diversified over the whole market!

357

In order to prevent your shares from plunging indefinitely when prices tumble, set a stop-loss order!

358

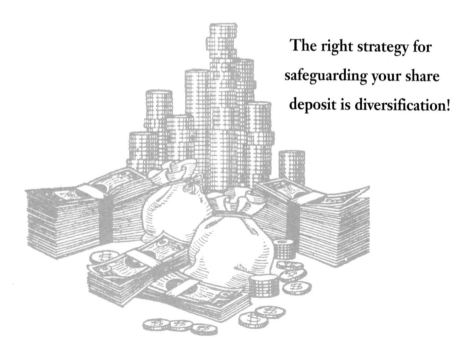

The right strategy for safeguarding your share deposit is diversification!

359

In spite of generally favourable stock market developments over several years, individual shares remain a risky investment for every investor.

360

Experience has shown

that the bond market

reacts to monetary and cyclical economic trends

much faster than the stock market!

361

Never invest your total assets exclusively
in shares and equity funds.
An optimal investment mix includes
investments in fixed-interest securities to cover short-term needs,
and if you are so inclined, participation in real estate.

Like the ocean, the stock
exchange is never still.
Philip L. Carret
If you cannot live with
the turbulence, you should not
invest in the stock market.

362

363

Short-term trading may lead to a fast and taxable profit.
More can be gained by a long-term continuous increase in value.

364

You can earn a lot of money with equity funds
only if you have the time to let your investment work for you.

365

If you have a lot of money,

you may invest at the stock exchange.

If you have no money,

you must invest at the stock exchange.

André Kostolany